State of Vermont
Department of Libraries
Northeast Regional Library
RD 2   Box 244
St. Johnsbury, VT 05819

Y0-BFI-641

Sweden

Sweden is the fourth largest country in Europe, covering an area of 450,000 square kilometers (174,000 square miles). There are about 96,000 lakes and more than half the total land surface is covered by forest. The northern part of Sweden is within the Arctic Circle and the area south of the arctic is sparsely populated. Most of the eight million people live in the south of the country.

Sweden is one of the world's leading industrial nations. Its wealth is based on abundant natural resources in the form of mineral deposits, forests and hydro-electric power. The country has large deposits of iron ore, and Sweden is a major exporter of iron and other mineral ores.

Manufacturing industries include engineering, steel, forestry (Sweden is the world's largest exporter of pulp for paper) chemicals, glass and china.

The people of Sweden enjoy one of the highest standards of living in the world, and in *We Live in Sweden* a cross section of Swedish people – young and old – tell you what life is like in their country; in the cities and the forests, in industry, in schools, at home.

Stephen Keeler is a teacher and lecturer in education and a writer of educational materials. He has lived and worked in Sweden for many years.

USSR

Kiruna

Jokkmokk

Luleå

FINLAND

GULF OF BOTHNIA

NORWAY

Mora

Rättvik

Falun

Börlange

Västerås

Uppsala

STOCKHOLM

Strängnäs

Lake Vänern

Lidköping

Mariestad

Skövde

Borås

Gothenberg

GOTLAND

Falkenberg

Orrefors

Kalmar

OLAND

DENMARK

BALTIC SEA

Malmö

we live in SWEDEN

Stephen Keeler
and
Chris Fairclough

The Bookwright Press
New York · 1985

Living Here

First published in the United States in 1985 by
The Bookwright Press, 387 Park Avenue South,
New York NY 10016

First published in 1984 by
Wayland (Publishers) Ltd
49 Lansdowne Place, Hove
East Sussex BN3 1HF, England

© Copyright 1984 Wayland (Publishers) Ltd

All rights reserved
ISBN: 0-531-03833-5

Library of Congress Catalog Card Number: 84-72080
Printed in Italy by G. Canale & C.S.p.A., Turin

Contents

"That's about half a million horses I've painted"

Birgit Johansson lives in Nusnäs — a small village near Mora. She is 38 and works for one of the many small, family firms in the area which make the world-famous wooden Dalarna horses. Birgit paints the bright, traditional designs on to the carved horses.

The story of the Dalarna horse is a simple one. In this part of Sweden wood is very important. We have a very big paper industry here. Paper, of course, is made from wood. Today, the paper industry is highly automated and efficient, but at the beginning of this century it was quite common for men to spend many months working deep in the huge forests, often far away from their homes and families. It was a lonely life for them, especially during the lengthy Scandinavian winters. In the long, dark nights they would often sit around a fire telling stories among themselves and talking about their wives and children. As they talked, they often whittled away at pieces of wood with their sharp knives, usually making toys to take home with them. The horse was an important working animal in those days. It was also a much simpler shape to carve than an elk, for instance. These men were lumberjacks, not fine craftsmen.

Today there are several different styles of wooden horse in Dalarna, but our orange-painted one is perhaps the best-known around the world. This is now

Cutting out the wooden horses with a band saw. Dalarna horses are quite a big industry.

quite a big industry. We export about 30 percent of our horses to the United States – to Minnesota, for example, where many Swedish immigrant families live.

The small horses are made from a single piece of pine. The larger ones are made from up to ten pieces which are firmly glued together. The basic shape is cut out on a band-saw and then the horses are sent out to different people for carving. Almost everyone in Nusnäs carves wooden horses. When they come back to the factory, the horses are dipped in the bright orange paint. This particular color of paint is made especially for us at a factory in Mora.

After the first coat of paint has dried, any cracks in the wood are filled with a kind of putty, and then the horse is given

Birgit can decorate a medium-sized horse in less than three minutes, but one this size takes up to fifteen minutes to paint.

a second coat of paint. Now my work begins.

I rub down each horse with a little linseed oil. Then I paint the design directly on the horse. There are no pencil lines to guide me, and I have to get it right first time. We use oil paint so that different colors don't run into each other. I paint about 70 horses each day, on the average. I've worked here for 21 years. So that's about half a million horses I've painted.

The oil paint takes two days to dry. Finally, the painted horses are given a coat of varnish to protect the paint and make them glossy.

"I love the silence and the stillness of the forest"

Bengt Wikman is 31. He lives in Näset, a small, remote settlement in the forests of Dalarna. Bengt builds wooden houses for a living, and when he's not working he enjoys playing traditional Swedish fiddle music.

You have to be an artist to live out here — an artist in the art of survival that is. There are no jobs here, no factories, no offices, not even any shops. The nearest town is Rättvik, about 40 kilometers (25 miles) away.

Hundreds of elk live in the forest, and sometimes they come up to the house — especially in winter. They're enormous, but they're not usually dangerous. They're also very tasty! There are bears and wolves too, but we very rarely see them. We can travel over 300 kilometers (186 miles) north from here, almost to the Soviet Union, without seeing a single house.

I love the silence and stillness of the forest. In winter the snow is sometimes 3 meters (10 feet) deep. We have to fetch our drinking water from the well. There are no movies and we don't even have a television — we don't need it. I'd never move to the town. The children learn so much here. They look after our five black sheep, and Anna, my wife, collects herbs for medicine — she makes wonderful herb teas. I build wooden houses and log cabins. It's a wonderful life, really!

In Näset we all work together, which

Bengt uses a chain saw for heavy cutting, and various axes for finer work.

saves money. If I need help with a house, our neighbor, Lasse, comes over. Then if he needs help with his car or someone to look after his kids, we lend a hand. We make almost everything we need ourselves; that way we can live on very little. When I've finished a house we can manage for maybe two or three months on what I get paid for it.

I'm well known around here. If someone wants a log cabin or a wooden house built they contact me and we discuss a price. Then I go out and buy the trees. My father, who lives nearby, has a timber truck and delivers the trees to me. I make the house in our backyard. It can take three or four weeks. The important thing is to get all the joints perfect — the logs must fit together without any gaps. When the house is finished I dismantle it and the owner calls to collect it.

We don't work more than we need to. We don't really want regular jobs. The government prefers people to live in the towns, and they only really give help to city people. If I wanted a job I'd have to move to a town. We've cut down our needs and we can live on very little, so we can make the most of nature.

When I'm not working on a house there's still plenty to do. Repairing our own house, mending fences, planting a few subsistence crops, helping our neighbors, all takes time. We have no time for anything else, like watching TV, for example.

Sometimes, in the summer, though, if there's no work to be done, we'll spend the day playing music. We usually begin in the afternoon. In Midsummer it doesn't get really dark for about four or five weeks here, and so sometimes we continue playing and dancing in the fields all night long.

Sweden is sometimes known as "The Land of the Midnight Sun" because the sun never sets completely during Midsummer in the far north.

"I'm a Lapp first and a Swede second"

Henrik Kuhmunen is a Swedish Lapp. He is 56 and he comes from Jokkmokk, just inside the Arctic Circle. He follows the traditional Lapp occupation of reindeer herdsman.

I can't say Lapland is my country. Lapland isn't a country. It has no borders and no government. There are no Lapp passports and no Lapp money. Lapland is an area. It crosses international borders. There are Lapps – or, as we call ourselves, *Sami* – living in much the same way and speaking much the same language in Norway, Sweden, Finland and the Soviet Union. I'm a Lapp first and a Swede second. I can speak Swedish, but my *Sami* is better. Yes, we have our own language – *Sami* – and it's completely different from other Scandinavian languages.

Henrik among his reindeer.

When my oldest daughter was born we were still nomads. The whole family used to follow the reindeer herds down the mountains in the spring. So my daughter went to a nomad school, where she learned to speak good *Sami*, and to sew leather and milk reindeer.

Very few Lapps are still nomadic – they don't move with the reindeer as they used to. When my father was a herdsman, my family used to live with the herd. They drank reindeer milk, wore clothes made from reindeer skins, and followed the herds on their annual migrations. They lived in tents, and when it was time to move on, they packed up everything on to the backs of a few animals and set off for the summer pastures.

We live in a house now, in Jokkmokk, and my younger children go to a normal state school. They don't learn *Sami* there but have local radio and TV programs in the Lapp language. I think I speak *Sami* better than my children and they speak better Swedish than I. My wife is a housewife now and my oldest daughter works in a store. I still work with the reindeer.

Nowadays, the reindeer are left to roam in enormous herds. We don't move them and follow them as we used to. Lapps mostly use aircraft and snowmobiles for reindeer herding, although a few are still nomadic and actually live with their moving herds. I think it's true to say that all reindeer breeding is now done solely for the production of meat. Reindeer meat tastes very good!

There are maybe 50,000 Lapps living in Northern Europe. About 15,000 of us live in Sweden. Since the population of Sweden is around eight million, that means that about one person in every five hundred is a Lapp. I think the Swedish government has tried to be very fair with

Lapp traditional handicrafts, such as knives, clothes and jewelry fashioned from wood, horn and leather, are very popular.

us, but many Lapps feel that our problems are ignored in Stockholm.

Our biggest problem is the gradual loss of our traditional reindeer breeding grounds. More roads have been built, opening up our lands to traffic, and tourists. Hydroelectric power plants have been built and intensive forestry projects are spoiling much of the land we have always regarded as our own. Wolves and bears are now protected animals. We mustn't hunt them because their numbers are threatened, but these animals do enormous damage to the herds.

We feel that our traditional occupation – reindeer herding – is threatened. Already our lifestyles have changed dramatically in the last fifty years. If the reindeer herds are constantly reduced, our cultural identity will disappear.

"We must be able to protect our neutrality"

Mats Green comes from Falkenberg. He is 20, and in common with most young men in Sweden, is doing his 15 months compulsory military service. Mats' cavalry regiment is based in Skövde but, like all regiments in the Swedish army, it occasionally provides the guard at the Royal Palace in Stockholm.

Sweden is not a member country of NATO – or of any other military alliance. Sweden has been neutral for around two hundred years in times of war. But this doesn't mean that we don't need an army. In fact, it means the opposite. If we don't belong to any military alliance, then we must be able to defend ourselves completely and protect our neutrality, because if we were to be attacked we would have no allies we could call on to help us. So we need large and powerful military services.

But Sweden has a tiny population – it's about the same as that of London. We haven't got enough people to support a large army. Therefore, it is necessary for everyone to be able to use weapons if they

During his military service Mats is allowed free rail transportation anywhere in Sweden.

have to. That's why military service for men is compulsory here.

The normal period of military service is 15 months, but you can opt for weapon-free service if you are a pacifist. In such cases you would work with telecommunications or in a hospital, kindergarten or some form of social work. The normal military service starts with several weeks of basic training – drill, marching, handling weapons. Then they send us out into the forests in the middle of winter for military exercises. In this part of Sweden temperatures can be as low as −20°C (−4°F) at that time of year!

You're supposed to begin military service on leaving school or college, but you can postpone it for a year or so if you've just started a new job. By law your employer has to release you and keep your job open until you return. After completing the 15 months you may be called to a three-week refresher course once every four years.

My regiment is called K3, which means the third cavalry regiment. We have three cavalry regiments but only one – K1 – still has horses, and they're only used for ceremonial occasions. We're really an infantry regiment now.

Almost every regiment in Sweden gets the chance to provide the guard here at the Royal Palace at least once a year. So that means that most Swedish men have done what I'm doing now. I suppose it's rather special. Many people are very proud to have guarded the Royal Palace. At any rate, it's a pleasant change in our routine.

Our king, Carl XVI Gustaf, and Queen Sylvia don't live here any more. The Palace is right in the middle of the city and there are no gardens or playgrounds, and very little privacy for the royal family. They moved to Drottningholm Palace – to the southwest of Stockholm – a few years ago.

My military service is almost over. I'm looking forward to leading a normal life again. I don't think many people really enjoy their military service, but most accept the need for it. We're usually free most weekends and we get about four weeks' paid leave during the 15-month period. But I get very little pay. You get more if you are married. We do get free rail passes, though, so I often go home to Falkenberg on weekends. Soon I'll be going home for good and will have to start thinking about a job.

Mats' regiment, wearing green berets, are relieved of duty at the changing of the guard ceremony outside the Royal Palace.

"Our Danish pastries are better than those in Denmark"

Ulla Bender is 53. She lives in Mora where, with her husband and their two sons, Leif and Mats, she runs the family *konditori*.

Every Swedish town has its *konditori* — an all-in-one bakery, confectionery and coffee shop — and we believe ours is one of the oldest shops in Mora. Certainly it's the oldest *konditori*. It opened in 1915 and has been in our family for the last quarter of a century.

A *konditori* usually has a shop in front, where you can buy bread and cakes, and a back room with tables and chairs, where you can have coffee and cakes or an open sandwich. You order your food and pay for it in the front shop. Then you take it through into the back room where there is always freshly-made coffee and you can have as many cups as you like without paying any more. Coffee and *Vienerbröd* (a cinnamon bun) cost around nine kronor (U.S. $1.08). Coffee and an open sandwich are about twenty kronor (U.S. $2.40).

In the summer we open up our garden behind the shop. That's very popular, especially with the tourists. We get a lot of German tourists in Sweden. They seem to love our cakes and instead of having one cake and several cups of coffee, they often have several cakes and one cup of coffee!

We used to serve our coffee in the traditional Swedish copper kettles but people

A mid-morning break at Ulla Bender's konditori.

Small settlements like this surround Mora. The traditional red-painted wooden houses and log cabins are seen throughout the country.

used to steal them. We still have one copper kettle but we only keep it for display. All our bread, pastries, cakes and sandwiches are homemade in the bakery. My husband is a master baker and confectioner. Leif helps with the cakes and Mats specializes in making open sandwiches. We try to keep to traditional styles and recipes, although we have invented a few new recipes for cakes. Our main concern is for quality. It's very important to have good cakes and bread. Our business has survived because of our high-quality goods. We like to think that our Danish pastries are better than those in Denmark!

In the larger cities many *konditoris* have closed down. There's a lot of competition there from fast food shops and from snack bars. Only the best are able to survive. Here in Mora our *konditori* is a meeting place for young people who perhaps come in for one coffee and sit for an hour chatting. Many people come into Mora from the surrounding villages and settlements to do their shopping and then come in for coffee and cakes while they're waiting for the return bus. We have a lot of regular customers who drop in on their way home from a training session at the sports center, or who meet their friends here before going on to an evening class.

"Each glass is an anonymous work of art"

Karl-Henry Fors is a master glass blower. He works at the world-famous Orrefors factory in the heart of the Swedish glass country. He is 49 and lives in the village of Ekaryd, about 40 km west of Kalmar, in the southeast of Sweden.

Over 90 percent of all Swedish glass is made in the area around Orrefors, in the province of Småland. At the end of the last century a small bottle works was opened at Orrefors. In those days, everything needed for glassmaking was available in the district – water and fine sand from the lake, and trees for the furnace fires. Today, for high quality crystal, we import a finer sand from Belgium and Britain, and of course the furnaces no longer burn wood. Other ingredients for glassmaking include potash, lead oxide, saltpeter and arsenic.

This factory employs fewer people than when I started working here twelve years ago, but we produce much more glass now. Machines are taking over many of the more laborious tasks. But every glass is still handmade – each one is slightly different and therefore unique.

It only takes a few seconds for me to shape a drinking glass. Molten crystal shouldn't be handled too much. That's why we make thin and delicate items, like these long-stemmed wine glasses, in the

Karl-Henry's team can produce around 150 hand-made wine glasses per hour.

mornings. The crystal is always better then, before it's been touched. Once it's shaped it cannot be altered. You could say that each glass is a work of art. An anonymous work of art, though, because the blower's name is never known. You could pick up a crystal bowl and recognize it as, say, designed by Olle Alberius (a famous designer), but you can never pick up a bowl and say, "Oh, this was blown by Karl-Henry Fors."

At the beginning of the century, the glass blowers and their assistants used the factory as a second home. In the long, freezing winters it was always warm, because of the furnaces. They used to bring food and prepare their meals here. Some even slept here. Even today we feel very attached to the place, and we often stay on in the factory long after normal working hours.

We work in teams of six – one master blower and five other workers. I have a good team; we work together in rhythm like a machine. When we're working there should be no hold ups. This means that we have to work at a speed which suits everyone. We work for 55 minutes and then take a five-minute break and we have a half-hour midmorning break.

The factory is always full of tourists in summer. Over 600,000 tourists visit Orrefors each year and working here becomes a sort of continuous demonstration. But we don't mind. It encourages us to take extra care and pride in our work, and it's good for business. Every American tourist wants to return home with some Swedish crystal. In fact, the United States is our biggest export market. 50 percent of our entire production is for the home market. Of the remaining 50 percent, about half goes to the United States and most of the rest goes to Australia.

There is a showroom and shop here and we always hope that people will look at the glass in a different way after seeing the lengths to which we go to produce the very highest quality crystal. People complain far less about our very high prices once they have actually been here.

Karl-Henry shapes the bowl of a wine glass out of molten crystal which cools rapidly as he works.

"I'm trained for anything that might happen"

Katarina Farmstedt-Wirén is 30. She lives and works in Malmö — on Sweden's southernmost tip — where she drives a police patrol car.

Here in Sweden we have one national police force. All trainees spend one year at the Police High School in Stockholm, followed by two more years of on-the-job training; one year in a police station, and the other out on the streets. During these

On the waterfront at Malmö, Katarina radios in and waits to receive instructions.

two years, trainees work with experienced police officers and sample the whole range of police work.

After my three years' training, I was appointed to the squad car division. Squad car officers work in pairs, and my partner and I have worked together now for five years. We have to get on well and build up a good working relationship. We need to rely on each other one hundred percent.

We're armed, of course. I wouldn't do this job without a gun. I wouldn't feel safe. I was very surprised to hear that the British police don't carry guns as part of their normal equipment. They must have some sort of security — they must be crazy! I don't go round shooting people, in fact I've never had to use the gun on duty, but I am prepared to use it if I have to, at any time. Knowing it's there is important to me. The criminals in Sweden know we're armed, and I believe it makes them think twice before committing serious and violent crimes. If we need more powerful weapons, machine guns for a terrorist siege for example, then we have to make a special application for them.

The most common offenses are traffic offenses. Everybody drives too fast. Here in Sweden you have to drive with dimmed headlights on at all times. The newer Volvos and Saabs have lights that come on automatically, and many modern foreign cars have been modified for Sweden in the same way. But even after eight years of this regulation we still have to stop motorists to tell them to switch their lights on.

Malmö is a quiet city, but then I guess Sweden is a quiet country, by international standards. Our work is probably very similar to that of police patrols throughout the world. We get called to discos when fighting breaks out, or to domestic quarrels where often the participants have had too much to drink. Young people with nowhere to go cause us a few problems, shouting in the streets or playing stereo radios too loudly. Our job is usually to calm people down; to talk to them and to try to persuade them to go on their way quietly. All the dramatic gunfire and the car chases are strictly for the movies – thank goodness!

When we're on duty we're equipped with a pair of handcuffs, and a key, billy club, a flashlight, a notebook and pen, a radio receiver/transmitter, and of course a pistol. And that's usually all we need. Most police work is routine. There are times when I feel uncomfortable. For instance, I don't like having to go into dark buildings alone and at night, although I'm quite prepared for anything that might happen. That's what I'm trained for. Maybe like my husband, who's a fireman, I get some kind of excitement out of a dangerous situation.

It's important that Katarina and her partner get to know as many people on their regular beat as possible.

"We like a bit of individuality"

Heikki Huotari's family originally came from Finland. Heikki, who is 22, now lives in Sweden, where he earns a living as a singer/guitarist with a Skövde band. All his spare time and money are spent on his car.

There are people like me all over Sweden. Big, old, flashy American cars are popular with us. Every town has its "motoring youth." That's what they call us, and it's not supposed to be a compliment. You see, in Sweden there's nothing for us to

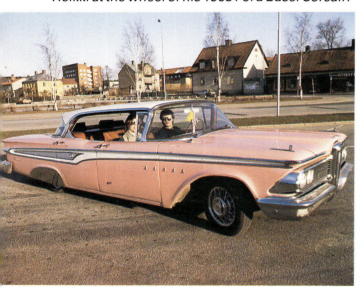

Heikki at the wheel of his 1968 Ford Edsel Corsair.

do. Unemployment is high and there are no places to meet. We don't have bars here, only restaurants where you must buy a meal if you want a drink. There's nowhere to just sit around and talk. Life is very safe here, very organized – very boring! Everyone has a nice house, a nice family, a nice car. Sure, Volvos are very good, but they're boring, to us, anyway. They're strong, safe, reliable – and they're all the same! And everybody has one!

We like a little bit of individuality. These fantastic automobiles are a symbol for us, I guess. We form clubs and have names like "Lidköping Roadmasters" or "The Skövde Superstars," and in each town there's an agreed route, usually around the center and through the market square, where we cruise round and round in the evenings. It's a little bit exotic – and it's a good feeling to be with others who think the same as us.

People stare at the cars, but I think they look at us for the wrong reasons. Sure, they're a little bit impressed, a little bit

Club members gather in a parking lot on the out-skirts of town, before beginning the evening cruise through the market square and around the town center.

envious too, but really they're scared of us. They think what they read in the papers about us is true and they expect us to stop and mug them and steal all their money. Ha! That's really crazy!

The police don't like us either. They're always stopping us and checking over the whole car. Everything has to be perfect. But we're not morons. We're real enthusiasts and almost all the cars are in excellent shape mechanically.

Mine is a 1968 Ford Edsel Corsair. I've had it for three years. The V8 engine gives it 290–300 horsepower. The car costs a lot of money to insure and repairs are very expensive too – one new tire costs about 1600 kronor (U.S. $192)! I only drive it for six months of the year. These cars were never built for Swedish winters. We put a lot of salt on our roads to prevent ice forming and it just eats away the car bodies. Most of us have our cars ready for

the road again by May 1st. I live near a very straight section of the E3 (European Highway 3) and I've had my car up to 190 km/h (118 m.p.h.) on that stretch. But generally we just cruise around town or visit another club.

We have just built ourselves a new clubhouse. We have music there and we can take a few cans of beer along and play table tennis or pool. It's really rather civilized, but most people think we're a bunch of hooligans who just drink and drive. Actually we never drink and drive. In Sweden you lose your license too easily for that. Instead of just sitting around complaining about how there's nothing to do, we've made something to do for ourselves.

"Only the weather is better in Turkey"

Jakup Dal is 43. He has lived in Sweden since leaving his native Turkey in 1976. He works in the foundry at the Volvo engine plant in Skövde.

I am an Armenian. I am also a Christian. As an orthodox Christian Armenian, I was in a cultural and religious minority in Turkey, and life was not always easy or safe there for me and my family.

My brother left Turkey for the Lebanon, but when the war started there he came to Sweden as an immigrant. I decided to join my brother, came to Sweden and lived here illegally for about six months until my claim to be a political refugee was accepted.

Now my whole family is here: my mother, my wife and our four children — three of them were born here in Sweden — my two sisters and their husbands, and my two brothers and their wives. Every Sunday we all attend the Swedish church, and the children go to Sunday School — all quite freely and without fear.

There have been no mixed marriages in our family yet – we have all married Turks, but we all have Swedish citizenship. Things will probably change, though, when our children grow up. It's much

easier for them to integrate because they spend all day at school with Swedish kids. They're beginning to forget what life was like in Turkey, and of course, they speak Swedish fluently. My Swedish isn't too bad either. When I first arrived here, I tried to teach myself Swedish from the newspapers. For the first month I couldn't understand anything. Then, suddenly, I began to understand a few things, and it got easier and easier. Then I started taking Swedish lessons. Every immigrant in Sweden has the right to a minimum of 240 hours of Swedish lessons, free of charge. Actually, I had lessons every day for three months — that's about 400 hours altogether. My mother tongue is Armenian Arabic, and we still use it at home sometimes, especially if we don't want the children to understand something. They don't speak any Arabic.

We've never been back to Turkey since we arrived in Sweden. Life here is easy for us, and I don't really miss anything. We eat Turkish food sometimes – there's

a special shop for foreign foods in Skövde, because there are many immigrant families living here – but usually we eat normal Swedish food, or sometimes a mixture. It doesn't matter. Here you can talk freely, contact people freely, make friends with whom you like and say what you want. It's good. Only the weather is better in Turkey! It was a little difficult to get used to the Swedish winters: the cold, and the long, dark nights.

I have a good job here and we live very well. Volvo is, of course, the biggest single employer in Skövde, which is actually quite a small town. That's one reason why so many immigrant families have been encouraged to come here. The company needed a large work force and there simply weren't enough local people to staff this huge plant. I work in the foundry, setting molds for engine castings. It's not a difficult job, and the working conditions are very good.

A newly-built Volvo engine arrives for testing on remote controlled conveyors, which move silently across the factory floor.

Jakup sets up the molds for the engine castings.

23

"You have to be good at everything in our schools"

Mia Sahlander is 16. She is a high school student from Falun, in her final year of school. When she leaves school she will attend domestic science college and then go to a catering school.

Our school system is divided into three sections, lower, middle and high. You can leave school at 16 but many people continue at either a gymnasium (a university prep school) or at technical vocational schools.

My final grades won't be good enough to get me into a gymnasium. But that doesn't matter. I've already decided to do a one-year course at our local domestic science college, and to follow that with a two-year course at a catering school. I want to work in a restaurant, initially as a waitress. The catering school has a restaurant in Falun where the trainees practice and where members of the public can get very cheap meals.

I like school. It's a nice place. Most of the teachers are very friendly and I have some good classmates. I study English, Swedish and math, which are all compulsory, German, natural sciences and humanities. English is my favorite subject and the one which will probably be of most use to me; it's also easier than German!

School starts at 8:20 a.m. and finishes

The celebration of "Lucia" – the Queen of Light – takes place on December 13. It is an honor to be chosen to play Lucia, as Mia was last year.

at 4:00 p.m. I have an average of six periods per day and get between five and six hours' homework per week. Going to classes is compulsory, but we do have free periods, and sometimes late starts and early finishes. We have a students' recreation room where we can read, play billiards or just sit around and chat.

I always have lunch at school. Every school in Sweden has to provide school meals and the local daily newspaper always publishes each day's menu. The food is not so good – the meatballs (a Swedish speciality) bounce on the table! But there's always plenty; it's self-service and you can eat as much as you like. School meals are provided free of charge in Sweden. Only the teachers pay, and they pay only a small amount. School lunch is a one-course meal but there are always vegetables and salad, milk, water or orange juice and crispbread with butter.

There are no exams in our school system. In some ways I think that's very good. You don't have to spend hours revising a year's work for one three-hour exam, and you don't need to get nervous and spend all summer worrying about results. But our system gives grades for every piece of work we complete during the year – it's called continuous assessment. This means you have to work consistently well during the whole year. That's OK. But the problem is that if you want to go to a gymnasium, or, after that, to a university, you have to have a top average grade. In other words, they put your grades from every subject together – even the subjects you dislike and don't want to continue – and then work out your average. If you want to get a high average grade it means you have to be good at everything in a Swedish school. One weak subject can ruin your chances.

Mia works on a project with a group of classmates.

"Winter begins at the end of August"

Erik Söderberg is 42. He comes from Luleå on the Gulf of Bothnia. He now lives in Kiruna in the far north of Sweden, where he works in the world's largest mine.

You have to talk in statistics to say anything about Kiruna. Sweden is the ninth largest exporter of iron ore in the world, and over 90 percent of that comes from Kiruna. If it weren't for the iron ore deposits there'd be no city at all up here, I'm sure. We're one hundred kilometers (62 miles) north of the Arctic Circle, on the same latitude as Alaska and Siberia. It takes almost twenty hours to get here from Stockholm by train. We are on the highway system, but once you get here the only place to go is back where you came from: all roads end in Kiruna! Our skiing season doesn't end until June, and winter is already beginning again by the end of August. And yet Kiruna is one of the biggest and fastest-growing cities of its kind in the world – although in 1890 there was only one log cabin here!

The Swedish mining industry is very varied: apart from iron ore, we also produce ores containing copper, lead, zinc and arsenic. We even have a little silver and gold here, and every year about 7 million tons of limestone are quarried, mainly for use by our cement industry.

Kiruna used to be well-known for its enormous open pit mining sites, but today most of the mines are deep underground. I am working in an iron ore mine which is almost 500 meters (1,600 feet) below ground level. Altogether we produce about 20 million tons of iron ore each year, and every day about thirty train loads of top quality ore leave Kiruna for the Norwegian port of Narvik, from which it is shipped to our customers in Europe.

The railroad line was opened in 1903. Although Narvik is well inside the Arctic Circle – it's north of Kiruna – the harbor remains open throughout the year because of the warm Gulf Stream. The Baltic freezes over completely even as far south as Stockholm, where the shipping routes between Sweden and Finland are kept open artificially by icebreaking ships.

The biggest importers of Swedish iron ore are West Germany, which buys almost a quarter of our entire production, France, which buys about a fifth, and Belgium and Luxembourg which together import about 19 percent.

Mining began here around the end of the last century. The mines were small and privately owned. Today they are massive, modern and entirely state-owned. We have some of the most sophisticated mining equipment in the world up here, and the standards of safety for the workers are very high.

With the exception of Murmansk in the Soviet Union, Kiruna is the most northerly city in the world. But for most of the year it's very quiet up here. During the short summer the character of the city changes completely for a few weeks. The midnight sun can be seen from the end of May until the middle of July, and quite a lot of tourists come here then. After they've all gone away, the place returns to its usual isolation.

Large scooping vehicles like this are used even in some of the very deep mines.

The landscape of the mining city of Kiruna.

"In Bombay I was a lecturer – here I'm nothing"

Hardika Hindocha is Indian, although she was born in Dar-es-Salaam in the African country of Tanzania. She has a British passport, a Ugandan Asian husband who is now a Swedish citizen, and two children who were born in Sweden, where the family has lived since 1977. She is 36.

In 1973 the president of Uganda, Idi Amin, expelled thousands of Ugandan Asians. Although of Indian origin, most of those expelled had been born in Uganda and were Ugandan citizens. Most were prosperous merchants with their own businesses, or successful professional people such as doctors, architects and lawyers. Overnight, Idi Amin made them not only homeless and virtually penniless, but also stateless – without a legal nationality.

The United Nations set up camps for the Ugandan Asian refugees, and my husband, who was driven out by Amin, made his way to one of these camps in Austria with less than U.S. $40 in his pocket, which was all he was allowed to take. The refugees had to leave all their savings behind. With this small sum my husband had to look after himself, his parents, his brother and his sister, who were expelled with him. The only possessions they were allowed were a few clothes.

This was before we were married. I was living in Bombay where I was a college lecturer. I was very worried at first, but when I knew that my husband-to-be was safe in a UN reception camp I felt relieved. Commissioners from many countries visited the camps and invited some of the refugees to come to their countries to settle and make new lives. My husband was invited to Sweden. After a year and a half he wrote to tell me he was coming to Bombay to marry me, and I knew that I would have to move to this country.

In Uganda my husband was a successful insurance broker – here he works in the packing department of an electrical appliances factory. In Bombay I was a college lecturer – here I'm nothing!

My husband is now a Swedish citizen and so are my two children, who were born here. I still have a British passport, but now that I have been living in Sweden for more than five years I can apply for Swedish nationality, which I will do soon.

Learning to live here has not been easy. I was brought up and educated for a life of relative ease and prosperity in Uganda.

Life is very different for Hardika, in Sweden. In Uganda she was used to status, money and servants.

Here I have to do everything myself. Swedish wasn't too difficult to learn. I speak it quite well enough and my children speak it perfectly. But the winters are so cold here and it's very difficult to get the food we are used to. Asian relatives in England send us food occasionally and there's a good shop in Jönköping where we can get spices and some fresh food, but it's very expensive.

Altogether about fifty Ugandan Asian families came here. I suppose the Swedish government has been very good to us. We were provided with jobs, places to live, free Swedish lessons and help with any settling-in problems we had. They even started showing a few Indian movies at the local theater! But we are such a tiny minority here. We live in a fairly enclosed community, and we have very few Swedish friends.

Hardika brews masala tea by boiling tea in milk and adding masala, a spice which tastes like cinnamon.

29

"Vicars work all week, not just on Sundays"

Roland Persfjord is 45. He comes from Nyköping but now lives in Falun where he is the Lutheran parish vicar. Besides church work he runs many activities and has fifteen assistants.

By the age of fourteen I knew I wanted to be a clergyman. So choosing school subjects and selecting a university course were easy! At high school I was able to study both Latin and Greek, which I needed in order to be accepted at the University of Lund, in southern Sweden, where I studied theology for five years. I was ordained at Strängnäs in 1966.

Ordination means being accepted into the Church as a clergyman, and is a ceremony which comes at the end of a period of formal study. I had taken my degree in theology and had been examined, orally, by a church council and by a bishop. I had to pass these oral examinations before being ordained, in Strängnäs Cathedral.

On an average Sunday about fifty people attend the service at Roland's church.

After my ordination I was assigned to the Cathedral at Strängnäs as an assistant. My bishop wanted me to do a kind of apprenticeship before being given a parish of my own. After a year at Strängnäs, this parish became available and I've been here ever since.

About 50,000 people live in the parish, but unfortunately only a small proportion attend church regularly. My salary is paid by those who live in the parish. Part of their annual taxes are paid to the State Church which then distributes the money to clergymen as a monthly salary. If anyone objects to their taxes being used for such purposes – they may have different religious beliefs, for example – they can apply to have their annual tax contributions reduced.

Religious education is the only subject on the school curriculum in Sweden which is compulsory. Although our state Church is Lutheran, religious education in our schools is not only about the Lutheran Church but about all major world religions. At my parish church we have special children's groups during the week for those especially interested in the Lutheran faith. Because so many people live in the countryside around Falun we found it difficult to collect sufficient children together on Sundays to support a Sunday School. Weekday evenings are much better because the kids come into Falun for school and it is much easier for them to stay for an extra hour or so. We teach them about Christianity, sing songs – we have four choirs for young people – and spend quite a lot of time outdoors during the summer months, including a summer camp.

Roland chats with his church organist after the service on a bright, spring Sunday morning.

There's a lot more to being a vicar than working on Sundays. I have a lot of paperwork to do, and that's the part of my job I dislike most. There are weddings, funerals, baptisms and, of course, confirmation classes. In Sweden, confirmation is very important. Around 65 per cent of all the thirteen- and fourteen-year-olds in Falun attend our confirmation classes. We even have special confirmation camps in the summer.

There are school visits, hospital visits and a whole range of church social events to carry out. I have fifteen assistants, so I'm also a boss! That means that whenever I want to change someone's job description or hire another person I also have to meet and discuss it with the trade unions. Yes, in Sweden we even have trade unions in the Church.

"We want a living community in the Old Town"

Karin Feltzin has been working as a freelance graphic artist for the past 32 years. Her studio is next door to her apartment in the picturesque Old Town in Stockholm. She is 58.

I studied commercial art, as it used to be known (it's called graphic art now), in Stockholm for four years. My first job was as a trainee in an advertising agency. When I wasn't making coffee for everyone I worked on movie posters. They were

Karin works in her studio, which is next door to her apartment in Stockholm's Old Town.

used for one week and then thrown away! But it was really valuable training for me. In those days there were no sophisticated mechanical aids. The lettering all had to be done by hand. Even today my hand lettering isn't bad although I never use it now.

My sons were born in 1953 and 1956. I had to stop going to work of course. At that time there were no day care centers. If you had young children you had to stay home and look after them. After about three months I was craving for work again, so I took on a little bit at home. It wasn't easy, but gradually I developed a system. As I was just beginning, I naturally took every job offered, believing it to be the last one I'd ever get! When any of the well-known illustrators took a vacation, that was the time to get my foot in the door as a new illustrator. My career has developed like that, through contacts. That's how it is when you freelance.

Most of my work in recent years has been illustrating science textbooks — mainly biology – for schools. I've designed wallcharts, posters and educational slides, as well as drawings and diagrams to illustrate texts. There are no schools for medical artists in Sweden so sometimes I have to watch postmortems at the pathology laboratory. It's often the only way to find out what a particular organ really looks like.

Ten years ago I was lucky enough to get this apartment in the Old Town. People who visit me always ask, "How did you get such a wonderful apartment?" But in those days it was easy. Everyone wanted a comfortable modern home, not a five-hundred-year-old apartment in the Old Town without hot water and with a toilet shared by four families. I live on the fifth floor and there's no elevator.

The apartments were renovated twenty-three years ago and central heating was put in. Recently the City Council took on responsibility for the Old Town and now there's a large renovation program under way. All the buildings are to be restored to their original exterior designs, and the apartments will be refurbished. I'll get hot water and an elevator – climbing those steep, stone stairs every day doesn't get any easier! The Council is trying to encourage families to move back into the Old Town, to reestablish a sense of living community. They also want "useful" people to live here – artists, craftspeople, bakers, shoe repairers – to retain the atmosphere of the Old Town. I think it's very good that they're not just interested in exploiting the Old Town financially. After all, they could easily renovate the apartments and fill the place with rich business tycoons. That would kill the place and it would become a kind of ghetto. It's much too valuable to us to let that happen to it.

The main market square in the Old Town.

"I can never relax as a passenger"

Irmgard Johansson is 52. She was born in Germany but married a Swede in 1951 and now lives in Gothenburg where, since 1967, she has driven streetcars and buses. She is also a city guide.

Gothenburg is the only remaining city in Sweden with a complete streetcar system. But there are certainly no plans to scrap it. Quite the opposite, in fact. The city has recently invested a great deal of money in a newly-designed streetcar which will eventually replace all those now operating.

Another fairly recent improvement was copied from an experiment carried out in Bremen, West Germany, where they installed special traffic lights which could be operated by the conductor from inside the cab. Now, for example, I can activate the lights at a crossing as I approach it, to keep pedestrians off the tracks. It means we don't have to keep slowing down at every pedestrian crossing.

In some European countries streetcars are regarded as old-fashioned and primitive. Our system is neither. It's quite sophisticated. In the past, conductors had to lean out of a window to change the points with a long pole. Now that's all done electromagnetically, at the flick of a switch. If I want to deposit sand on the tracks I can also do that by pressing a button. Sand is needed to give better traction

Irmgard talks to a passenger outside the streetcar company office in Gothenburg.

if the tracks are very wet, or at the bottom of a hill. It's a pity no one's invented a machine for filling up the sand boxes inside the streetcars! I still have to do that manually at the start of each shift. Even though we have quite bad winters here, ice and snow on the tracks aren't usually a problem since the whole streetcar system is heated.

Streetcars generally travel at around 35 km/h (22 m.p.h.), although they can go much faster. We have very few accidents, and our general safety record is good. But as an experienced conductor I can never relax as a passenger. I'm always as alert as if I were driving. If I hear something wrong with a door (streetcars cannot move unless all the doors are fully closed) I can tell that the compressor's faulty. Or if I smell something (the brakes are too hot!) I brace myself when I think the driver's going to need to use the emergency brakes. And then I look around the streetcar at the other passengers and notice that they're all relaxed and completely unaware of all these things! I guess you just can't enjoy a streetcar ride if you're a conductor!

We sometimes have problems with vandalism and fare evasion. To try to reduce the vandalism we started a program of school visits. Groups of children come to our head office and learn about the value of the streetcar system. They see models of old and new streetcars and carry out school projects on what they have seen. Some of their work is very good, and there is now less vandalism.

As for avoiding fares, most streetcars are linked in pairs and the rear car is usually unmanned. But we recently appointed a few more ticket inspectors and advertised this fact. Now even fare evasion is less common.

A Gothenburg city streetcar and bus at one of the central terminals.

"Artists are not often good throwers"

Göran Fogelqvist is 26. He lives in Lidköping where he works as a potter at Rörstrands, one of Sweden's best-known ceramics factories.

I came here right after leaving school. I'd always been interested in clay and thought it would somehow be rewarding to work with it. When you watch a master potter at work on the wheel it always looks so easy, but it isn't.

Hand-throwing fifty plates like this in one day is no problem for Göran.

When I first joined Rörstrands I did one year of basic training learning about the qualities of clay, the use of glazes and the effect of baking in the kiln. Then I started to work on some of the simpler bowls that we produce. In the ten years I've been here I've worked in most parts of the factory and know something about all the machinery and all the processes. I think it's very important to know what everyone else does, and also to be able to do it oneself. It makes for better understanding between workers in a large place like this.

I'm not a designer, and at the moment I have no particular interest in designing. I think you probably have to have a flair for it, and I don't think I've got that kind of imagination. So I work to someone else's designs and I'm happy to do so. Artists are not often good throwers (clay workers) anyway.

People often seem surprised to find pottery still being handmade at a large factory like this. But although we do produce very large amounts of crockery, using modern machine-aided techniques, we're not only interested in mass-production. In fact it's actually more economic to produce a small series of items, such as this order for fifty of these deep plates, by hand. To make a mold for a piece like this would take time of course, and then to set up the machinery to reproduce fifty plates would also take time. Then there's all the power used in operating the machine. I can make fifty plates by hand more quickly and very much more cheaply. These plates will sell for around 100 kronor (U.S. $12) each.

Hand thrown pots are unique. Even in this series of fifty, no two will be exactly the same. Here at Rörstrands I think they try to achieve a good balance between the use of machinery and the development of human skills. We sell tea and coffee cups to hotels and restaurants all over the world. We recently supplied crockery to Manchester Airport. That kind of thing is obviously machine molded. But if we take part in exhibitions, we like to display unique, handmade items.

Every year, in the second week of August, we hold a pottery throwing competition here in Lidköping. Master craftsmen from all the Nordic countries gather here to display their skills. The competition is to find the potter who can make the tallest vase and the widest plate or bowl from one standard, measured piece of clay. The potter who wins the first prize gets a free trip to Florence in Italy, where a similar competition is held. Perhaps next year I'll enter the competition myself.

A view across the factory floor showing the racks of machine-molded crockery.

"We have to be first to get the best price"

Gillis Nilsson is 65. He owns a large farm and a campsite on the island of Öland, where he has lived all his life. The farm specializes in producing early fruit and vegetables.

The climate down here is milder than almost anywhere else in Scandinavia. Summer temperatures often reach 35°C (95°F), and snow is a rare sight on Öland in winter. The climate is ideal for fruit and vegetables because the growing season is so much longer and late frosts are less likely. The good weather also makes this part of Sweden very popular with tourists. I divide my activities between farming and tourism.

This tractor attachment makes it possible for Gillis to plant five rows of lettuce at one time.

The farm takes more looking after than the campsite. We produce lettuce, strawberries, potatoes, brown beans and cucumbers. Planting starts between late March and mid-April, after the risk of overnight frost is past. We buy our lettuce plants from Denmark and cultivate them in mounds of specially warmed earth. We have a special attachment for the tractor which allows us to plant up to five rows of lettuce at a time. They still have to be harvested by hand, and they have to be ready for lifting by June 10. It takes no more than two days to transport and distribute them by road to all the major cities in southern and central Sweden. We send most of our lettuce crop to Stockholm, Västerås and Borås.

I've got one and a half hectares (3½ acres) of strawberries. They have to be ready by the Midsummer weekend, though. To get the best price we have to be first, and by using plastic sheeting to cover the strawberry beds we can harvest them up to fifteen days earlier than would be possible without plastic. Strawberries ready before Midsummer will fetch a good price, but immediately after the prices will slump and of course then we lose money on them. Strawberries picked here in the morning can be flown to Stockholm and be on sale there the next day.

The campsite opens on May 1 each year. That's a public holiday in Sweden (no matter what day of the week it falls on) and the start of the season for us in the southeast. I have thirty mobile homes and this year we've just built ten new log cabins at a cost of 55,000 kronor (U.S. $6,600) each. It will cost 1,500 kronor (U.S. $180) per cabin per week to rent one during the high season – that's during July – and 1,000 kronor (U.S. $120) per week in June and August. In the low season the rent is much lower.

Last year we had 50,000 visitors. There are boats available for campers, and, of course, they can pick their own strawberries. The season ends on November 31, and that's about the only time I get a chance to take a vacation. Last year my wife and I took a short winter vacation in England. We chose England so that I could go and inspect a mobile homes park there (I was thinking of buying some more English trailers for the camp site). So even on vacation I was still working.

I'm a little too old to have many ambitions left, but I'd very much like to sell strawberries to the Arabs. I'm sure it's possible to pick them today and have them on sale in Saudi Arabia tomorrow. Maybe next season.

Gillis unloads fresh crates of small lettuce plants ready for planting.

"The computer knows where I am – and tells me where to go"

Berit Aving is 36 and lives in a suburb of Stockholm, from which she and her husband run their taxi business. The new instruments on the dashboard of her car mean she no longer needs to go looking for customers.

It's my husband's business. He's the boss, and I work for him. We have two cars — both Volvos, of course! — although we only use one at a time. The other is kept as a reserve, in case of breakdowns.

I drive during the daytime. My husband won't allow me to drive at night. He takes over then. It's much safer that way, but it does mean that we don't see much of each other.

Actually, we don't have much trouble. Friday and Saturday nights are the worst. The main problem is with people who've had too much to drink, and that's quite a problem in Stockholm. Every taxi is fitted with a transparent plastic wraparound shield behind the driver's seat, which protects the driver against strangulation by crazy customers. That makes being a taxi driver sound like a really dangerous job, but Stockholm is actually a very safe city, and I've never had any serious trouble.

As a Stockholm taxi driver I can operate anywhere in the city, and occasionally I find myself at the taxi stand outside the Central Station. We don't have many taxi stands in Stockholm and it's still more common here to telephone for a taxi than to hail one on the street. Now that we have radio-activated printers in the cars we can be constantly busy. There is a Stockholm taxi data center which collects all reservations made by telephone anywhere in Stockholm. Each taxi has a computer identity number and the data center's computer distributes the work fairly between all the drivers working at any one time, depending on where in the city they are and whether or not they have a customer.

As soon as I finish a job, I tap out my number on the miniature keyboard in my car to inform the computer that I'm free. That way the computer knows where I am and can tell me where to go next. Usually there's a constant flow of jobs chattering out of my miniprinter on the dashboard. Even if I have to take someone a long way out of the city center, the computer will usually find me a return fare so that I don't have to waste time and gasoline by coming back to town with an empty car.

Traffic regulations are very strict in Sweden. Speed limits are low – the fastest, 110 km/h (68 m.p.h.), being reserved for thruways and a few stretches of major road. In 1967 we changed from driving on the left to driving on the right. That was a really sensible decision for us, since we had never had right-hand drive cars in Sweden and passing was always hazardous because we could never see clearly what was coming toward us. Generally, people obey the rules and the standard of driving is good – it has to be, in a country where for much of the year the roads are under ice and snow and driving conditions are dangerous. We use studded snow tires in the winter but they have to be taken off as soon as the last snow has gone because they cause terrible damage to the roads.

(below) *Berit's taxi cannot go down this ancient street in the beautiful Old Town, in the heart of modern Stockholm.*

(above) *Berit uses a few minutes between jobs to make sure her car reaches the high standards of cleanliness set by Stockholm taxi drivers.*

"We know that no one will bother to learn Swedish"

Barbro Carnehag is 34. She was born in Västerås but now lives in northern Sweden. She works in a high school where she teaches English and French.

I've been teaching for ten years. Before that I studied English, French and linguistics at Uppsala University, followed by a one year postgraduate teaching course – also at Uppsala. I'm very interested in teaching and try to attend as many in-service training courses as I can. People are always taking courses in Sweden – it's a national pastime!

I think we should always look for better ways to teach – especially English, which is one of the most important subjects in our curriculum. Since Sweden is such a small country we need a world language. We need to speak English because we know that no one will bother to learn Swedish just to speak to us. If we want to communicate with the rest of the world, we have to do it in English. Most of my students realize this, and fortunately, nearly all of them have a good grasp of English already.

Our children start school at the age of seven, although very many children go to a kindergarten from the age of four or five.

All my students call me Barbro – not Miss Carnehag. That would sound a bit odd in Swedish, and in any case I firmly believe that we should not try to create barriers between teachers and students. I want my students to think of me as Barbro, a person they know, not as a remote teacher.

Marking students' work gives me sleepless nights! Marks are very important here because, instead of examinations, we have continuous assessment. Of course we still have occasional tests but it's really the students' course work that counts, and the marks they get for their work determines whether or not they go on to college or a university or into some form of vocational training. You have to have a top grade just to get into a hairdressing course these days, and I know that giving my students low marks could seriously affect their careers. It's a terrible responsibility!

Discipline isn't a problem. Of course I don't work in a big city school in Stockholm. But even there it's not a real prob-

Classes are usually quite small in Swedish high schools.

lem. Nobody really cares much about discipline, and therefore it's not an issue. Of course I am disappointed if a student doesn't do his or her homework or fails to complete a piece of work. But if I have a good relationship with students they will want to avoid disappointing me. I think there's quite a well-developed sense of responsibility here.

Teaching hours and salaries are clearly laid down in Sweden. An elementary school teacher teaches 29 classes per week and is paid less than a middle school teacher who teaches 24 classes per week. Highschool teachers, like me, teach 21 classes per week and are better paid than middle school teachers.

In spring Barbro changes the tires on her car from studded snow tires to normal ones.

"There's a very high turnover of staff in hotels"

Gunilla Jacobsson is a receptionist at the Hotell City, in the center of Stockholm. Originally she came from Furudal, a small village near Rättvik. She is 24.

When I left school I got a job in a local store selling wallpaper, paint and floor coverings. It's sometimes very difficult for young people to find work in small villages. In a few years' time many of the villages in northern Sweden may be empty, like ghost towns, because all the old people will have died and the young ones moved to a town.

I didn't want to sell paint in a village store all my life. I wanted work that changes from day to day, contact with lots of interesting people, and to be able to choose where I worked.

I started searching through the advertisements in our national newspapers and found one from a Stockholm lady living in Spain, who wanted someone to help with the cooking and cleaning. I studied Spanish at school and I'd always wanted to work with languages (I also studied English, French and German). So I applied, got the job and went to Spain for just over a year. It was very good for my Spanish. There is really only one way to learn a foreign language properly and that's to go and live in a country where it's spoken.

I returned from Spain, enrolled in a course for people wanting to work in hotels (there are courses for everything in Sweden!) and then got my first job in a

Most of the guests are strangers to Stockholm and need advice and information about how to get around the city.

small Stockholm hotel. You need a good basic education, and to be able to speak several languages. English is essential. Then you need hotel "style," I mean you have to look like a hotel receptionist. It's difficult to define, but you have to look the part. Travel and living in other countries is also useful experience.

My job involves receiving guests, checking them in, giving information and answering the telephone. When guests arrive at a hotel in Sweden they have to fill in a registration form. We have to know exactly who the guests are. The forms go to the police, but aren't used except in specific police investigations. People normally reserve rooms in advance; very few just turn up without a reservation. The computer has taken over one of the receptionist's most laborious jobs — keeping room lists. Reservations are fed into the

Opposite the hotel is a market square decorated with tubs of spring flowers.

computer. Registrations, which confirm that a guest has arrived, are also fed in. Then, each day, the computer prints out a complete list of occupied rooms, free rooms, and rooms that need cleaning and preparation for the next guests. When someone checks out, the name is automatically removed from the daily room list, but the computer keeps a record of that person's stay at the hotel.

I like the unpredictability of the daily work. Hotell City is a busy downtown hotel in the heart of Stockholm. Unfortunately, I don't live in, which means I have to commute each day, but I like the job and I'll probably stay here for quite a while. There's a high turnover of staff in the hotel business, probably because there are so many interesting places to work.

"I play badminton every Friday morning before work"

Jonas Norrbom is 24. He was born in Småland and now lives and works in Gothenburg, where he is the manager of the sports department at one of Gothenburg's biggest department stores.

This store, Åhléns, began in Gothenburg in 1895. We now have a chain of a hundred supermarkets, called *Tempo*, through the whole of Sweden. There are two Åhléns department stores in the country, this one and our main store in Stockholm.

The store opens every weekday at 9:30 a.m. and closes at 7:00 p.m., except on

Jonas gift-wraps a customer's purchase.

Saturdays when we close at 4:00 p.m. We even open on Sunday afternoons in the fall. I started working here two years ago, when I moved to Gothenburg from Småland where I was born and brought up. It's the first and only job I've had. I'm quite ambitious, I think, and hope to become a section chief within two years.

Like most companies in Sweden, Åhléns has its own training department. Ever since I started working here I've been undergoing continuous training of one kind or another. After my initial training, which everyone gets, I was selected for buyer training. That means learning all about what my department sells at various times of the year, what the demand is for certain goods, how to estimate the amount of stock the department will need, and how to handle the buying budget. As manager of the sports goods department I'm responsible for making sure that we have fishing tackle in the spring, ice hockey gear in the autumn and soccer equipment in the summer (in Sweden our soccer season starts in early summer). We also sell camping equipment and general goods such as track suits, running shoes and swimwear. I'm responsible to our section chief who is in charge of a group of departments. That's the job I'd like some day.

We also have a voluntary and continuous in-service training program, in which I take part. Later this year I'll start on a six-month's training course at the store's own school in Stockholm. Three months will be spent learning about textiles and hardware, and the other three months I'll be working in our Stockholm store.

I don't play many sports myself, not even ice hockey, which is our national sport here in Sweden, but I love fishing and I also play badminton early every Friday morning before I start work. I don't really have the time for fishing any more. I like to get out of Gothenburg and return to Småland where I used to do quite a lot of deep-sea fishing. I occasionally fish for trout, perch and pike in the crystal clear lakes near my old home.

Department stores are pretty much the same everywhere in the world, but one thing you'll notice about a Swedish department store is that there is always a free gift-wrapping service. If a customer tells me that he or she is buying something as a present for someone, I'll wrap it in special gift paper and tie curled colored ribbon around it – all at no extra cost.

Jonas is an ardent fisherman. The lakes and forests of Sweden are a fishing paradise.

"Nobody likes being stopped by the customs officer"

Mats Hultberg is 27. He lives in Gothenburg – Sweden's second largest city – and works as a customs officer at the Skandia Harbor, where ferries dock daily from England and Holland, and where container ships arrive from all over the world.

We check about 10 percent of the cars coming off the ferries. Nobody likes being stopped by the customs officer. People don't like having their suitcases opened and their cars searched. So we try to be as low-key and polite as possible.

We find about one percent of dutiable goods among the ten percent which we check, and they are usually goods which are highly taxed in Sweden, such as wine and alcohol – especially whisky, which can cost over U.S. $20 a bottle here.

If I discover someone with an extra bottle of alcohol or a package of cigarettes over the limit, I may confiscate the excess and let them go. Up to eight bottles over the limit we regard as petty crime and there's a fixed scale of fines which have to be paid immediately. Beyond that, the penalties are much more severe and I can impose a fine based on a percentage of someone's salary if I find them smuggling large amounts of dutiable goods into the country.

We're not really interested in tourists or short-term visitors, although we do want to discourage them from breaking Swedish law, and we're always on the look out for narcotics and other illegal drugs. It's systematic smuggling we have to prevent. But with over 300,000 passenger arrivals per year at this harbour alone we have no real way of knowing how much we miss. We work closely with the passport and immigration control section, and the ferry company.

I don't work just at the ferry terminal; in fact that's quite a small part of my job. Skandiahamnen is Europe's biggest container harbor. Between 500 and 700 containers arrive each day here, and that means a lot of paperwork for the customs authorities! Once again narcotics are at the top of our list of illegal imports. A more common problem, though, is false descriptions of legitimate goods. For example, we may get a cargo of clothes from, say, Hong Kong, which are described as being made of cotton. On inspection we may find that they're made

of silk, and therefore much more valuable. The import duty will be much higher. The importer may have described them as cotton to avoid paying such a high import duty.

I also have to make sure that goods coming into Sweden are safe. We have strict laws about the safety of toys and electrical goods. Occasionally I have to turn back a consignment of toys which are made from inflammable material, or electrical goods which don't conform to our laws because they're not wired correctly or insulated properly.

It's an interesting and varied job, but the hours are often unsocial and it's poorly paid. Like most people in Sweden I love sailing, and ideally I would like my job to have something to do with the sea. I really wanted to be in the coastguard, but you have to have had two years experience at sea for that. The customs authorities and the coastguard service are very closely connected and it may eventually be possible for me to get a transfer.

Gothenburg is the biggest port in Scandinavia and one of the most modern in Europe.

Mats examines the luggage of a passenger who has just come off the ferry.

"Every year the world requires more and more paper"

Roald Borch Michelsen is a director of the Kvarnsveden paper mill at Borlänge. He is 60 and has worked in paper mills since 1947.

When people pick up their morning paper, they don't know who has made the news-print – the actual paper it's printed on. They probably don't care. The big paper-producing companies of the world don't advertise to the general public because it's not the general public who purchase the paper. Our purchasers are the publishers and printers.

Kvarnsveden Paper Mill is part of a much larger group of companies – Stora Kopparberg – which is one of the oldest companies in the world. Stora Kopparberg is Sweden's second largest forestry and forest-based products enterprise and one of the country's largest power producers. More than 75 percent of the sawn wood products, 80 percent of the pulp and 75 percent of the paper manufactured by the company in Sweden is exported – chiefly to European countries.

Logs tumbling through the debarking machine at an early stage in the papermaking process at Kvarnsveden.

Our mill has always been one of Europe's biggest producers of wood-containing printing papers and we specialize in the production of high quality newsprint. If you buy one of the popular newspapers printed in England, for instance *The Daily Mirror*, *The Daily Express* or *The Daily Telegraph*, or *The Daily Record* in Scotland, you'll almost certainly be buying Kvarnsveden paper. I say "almost certainly" because no publisher relies on one supplier only. That would be very unwise. Perhaps they also buy small quantities of Canadian newsprint. Canadian paper mills are our biggest competitors, and the competition is tough.

In an industry with such a limited market it doesn't make sense to have large numbers of companies fighting each other for the same customers. So we decided to join with three other Swedish and two Norwegian paper mills to form Press Papers Limited, which is a kind of marketing company which distributes the market share according to each mill's capacity and specialty. Press Papers Ltd. looks after all our interests.

This kind of organized compromise is a great advantage really. OK, so we at Kvarnsveden don't get all the market share, but we do get stability, plus regular customers and a steady flow of work. This has made it possible for us to plan with far greater accuracy, to avoid the risk of bankruptcy and to develop a highly specialized range of products which we know our customers want. In turn, this has made it possible for us to keep the price of our paper stable and to develop excellent working relationships with all our customers.

Every year the world requires more and more paper – 26 million tons last year, of

This tractor, with snow chains on the tires, has a saw on the lifting arm that can cut all the logs to the required size at the site.

which this factory produced around 450,000 tons. That's about 3,500 cubic meters (123,563 cubic feet) of newsprint per day, and we are currently building new equipment which will give us a capacity to produce around 530,000 tonnes per year.

"Sometimes I read two hundred books a week"

Gunilla Broberg is Head Children's Librarian at the public library in Mariestad. She is 40 years old, has three children of her own and some very definite views on what makes a good children's book.

Many people think that being a librarian means checking library cards, collecting fines on overdue books, and date-stamping the circulation slips. Of course, all that is part of library work, but being a librarian is much more exciting than that.

I first became interested in libraries when I got an office job in the Stockholm Public Library, after leaving Uppsala University, where I'd studied modern languages. When we had to move to Mariestad in 1975, I got a job as a library clerk. That's when you do all the card-checking and date-stamping!

A year later I enrolled in a full-time librarianship course in Borås for two years and in 1978 I returned to the library here as social librarian. It was a wonderful job because I was free to develop it in my own way and put my new ideas into practice. As social librarian I was responsible for making sure that old, handicapped or sick people living in Mariestad had access to any books they wanted from the library. They were usually unable to come to us, so I went to them. We have a mobile library bus, but that serves the more remote country districts around Mariestad. My

Gunilla likes to encourage children to come into the library even before they can read.

The public library at Mariestad.

job was much more than just messenger girl, bringing books from the library to those who couldn't collect them themselves. Often they needed information about new books or required reference materials.

It was during this period that I began to build up a collection of old books, documents, photographs and postcards relating to the province and the town. We soon had a room full of authentic, historical reference material which proved to be very popular with people trying to trace their roots and drawing up family trees.

I have recently moved from the social department to this new job of head librarian in the Children's Library. As head of department I have my own budgets and can realize more of my ambitions for the library.

Children's books are so important. They can have a very powerful influence on the way children grow up. We have to avoid buying new children's books just because they look bright and exciting. The language is very important – we make sure we don't stock books which are sexist or racist. A good book must deal with children's problems and try to offer honest solutions. Sometimes I read two hundred books a week because I don't want to buy anything for the library that I haven't read and approved myself.

If the kids don't come into the library, then I take the library to the kids – like I did when I was a social librarian. I have tried to develop good relations with most of the schools in Mariestad. I arrange suitable times with the teachers and then go into schools and talk to groups of pupils. I take lots of new books with me from which I read specially selected short passages – to whet their appetites. If they like the sound of any book, they can borrow it from me then and there and I'll collect it when I next visit the school.

"You have to provide a service for the tourists"

Berndt Sundberg is the Regional Director of Tourism for southeast Sweden. At 46 he has already spent nine years directing a large export agency. He's a civil pilot, a scuba diving enthusiast and an ardent golfer.

My interest in tourism began at an industrial exhibition. I used to be the director of an export agency which looked after the export interests of several small Swedish companies — each too small individually to spend large amounts of money trying to win export orders. My agency's job was to gather information about the export markets, to publicize the companies' products and to win orders from abroad on their behalf. We took part in many industrial exhibitions where we displayed Swedish products against enormously enlarged photographs of the Swedish countryside. I soon found many Japanese and German business people asking me, "Where is this? It looks magnificent, can we go there?"

So, in 1972, I moved to Kalmar to co-ordinate the activities of all the local tourist boards. Until then, each town in the region had had its own, separate tourist board. That was terribly inefficient. Öland is just across the bridge. It's no good saying, "I'll show you round Kalmar, but I can't take you to Öland, that's not my responsibility." So now we're a regional organization, with our head office here in Kalmar and a permanent staff of five. We cover an enormously rich and varied area of Sweden.

The bridge to Öland is more than six kilometers (nearly 4 miles) long and is the longest in Europe.

Berndt sometimes shows people round the town of Kalmar, where the castle used to be known as the "lock and key" of Sweden.

There's the "Glass Country," less than an hour away by bus; Kalmar itself with its magnificent castle and old town, and the impressive bridge to Öland. Öland is the major attraction of the region. Of the 28,000 summer houses in the area, 8,000 are on Öland. There are twenty-six authorized camping sites, and it's a paradise for botanists and ornithologists. There are millions of flowers, including thirty different kinds of orchid growing wild, and hundreds of different species of birds. For archaeologists there are forty old fortresses, some dating back to Viking times. At one time there were several thousand windmills on the island. There are still about four hundred remaining — some as working mills, though they're mechanized now. Others which have been renovated are open as restaurants or inns. The climate here is almost perfect, too. But even if it does rain there's still plenty to do.

Nowadays it's so easy to make a phone call from anywhere in the world. It's quite common to get a call from people in Holland, say, who want to know about the exact length of a boat they're going to charter here during their vacation. You never really know what's going to happen each day. Of course there are lots of meetings, but they often have to be canceled if something more urgent comes up. It's not good to have too many meetings. You have to be out there providing the service for the tourists, and I think it has to be run in the same way you'd run a business. People like to travel, but traveling is tiring; and at the end of each day, people expect their hotel, cabin or camping site to be clean, comfortable and welcoming.

"When news stories break we get them first"

Claes Astin is 52. He lives on the shores of Lake Vänern, in Mariestad, where he works as a reporter and broadcaster for the local radio station, Radio Skaraborg.

I came to Radio Skaraborg in 1980, three years after the station opened. Before that I was a TV news reporter for the western TV region.

We don't have an independent or commercial radio network or TV channel here in Sweden. Both our TV and all our radio channels are under the control of the two national broadcasting organizations, Sveriges Television and Sveriges Radio (*Sverige* is the Swedish word for Sweden). But, like many countries, Sweden is divided into several radio and TV regions, each of which provides local news coverage and makes programs about local issues.

There are 24 local radio districts in Sweden. Radio Skaraborg serves roughly the area of Skaraborgs Län. *Län*, in Swedish, means rural district or county. Our head office and studios are in Skövde, about 50 kilometers (30 miles) away. Here in Mariestad four of us run this little sub-station. Local radio stations are funded from the television license fee which, for

a color TV, is currently 270 kronor (U.S. $36) per quarter.

Of course we do broadcast national and international news, but we specialize in local stories, some of which we get from the county council and the regional schools administration which have their offices in Mariestad. We also record a lot of material for future use, such as local traditional music, interviews with local craftspeople in their workshops, and sports reports, which we buy from the local newspapers and from a teacher who works for us part time. Occasionally we send programs up to the national network and if they like them they may broadcast them across the whole country.

The whole point of local radio in Sweden is to give a voice to the community and to improve communication between sometimes remote country districts. With such objectives it's not really surprising that we are constantly competing against the local newspapers, and unfortunately our relations with them are not as good as

Claes, in the inner studio, presents a local news bulletin.

they could be. Perhaps they feel threatened by us – although I'm sure that most of our 270,000 listeners still buy a local paper too. Since Radio Skaraborg opened there has been no substantial drop in local newspaper circulation figures.

There are some things – not many! – that newspapers do better than radio. They have pictures. We have to rely entirely on words. But when local news stories break we get them first. We can broadcast a live interview. You can actually listen to someone speaking rather than read their reported words the next morning. We don't have to wait for tomorrow's print run.

A radio car and portable taperecorder mean that Radio Skaraborg can broadcast local news events as they happen.

Facts

Capital city: Stockholm.

Principal language: Swedish. All schoolchildren learn English as a second language.

Population: 8.3 million. 90% live in the southern half of Sweden. The country has a low birth rate. Since 1945 more than 600,000 immigrants, mostly from neighboring countries but also from other parts of the world – have accounted for more than half of the population growth. The Lapps, an ethnic minority with a reindeer-herding tradition, have lived in northern Sweden for thousands of years.

Climate: Sweden is the fourth largest country in Europe. Half its land surface is covered with forest and there are about 96,000 lakes. The land is flat except for a long mountain chain in the northwest with peaks up to 2,111 meters (6,926 feet) high. There are thousands of islands along the coast. The warm Gulf Stream in the Atlantic gives Sweden a milder climate than other areas equally far north. In the far north the winters are long and cold with snow lasting for up to 7 months. In June and July the sun never sets (midnight sun). Further south the summers are warm and sunny with milder winters and moderate snowfall.

Currency: 8.3 kronor = U.S. $1.00

Government: Sweden is a constitutional monarchy with a parliamentary form of government. The king, since 1973 Carl XVI Gustaf, has only ceremonial functions as Head of State. Parliament (*Riksdag*) consists of one chamber whose members are elected every 3 years. Everyone over the age of 18 has the vote.

Housing: Sweden has a very high standard of housing. Most families live in apartments which are built to meet very high standards.

Raw materials: Sweden has an abundance of natural resources, in the form of forests, mineral deposits and water power. Large deposits of iron ore are found north of the Arctic Circle in the area of Kiruna and Gällivare-Malmberget and also in southern Sweden, around Bergslagen. Sweden is a major exporter of iron ore, via the Norwegian port of Narvik, and through the Swedish ports of Luleå and Oxelösand. Other raw materials are copper ore, lead ore, zinc ore and minerals for aluminum.

Manufacturing industry: Sweden is one of the world's leading industrial nations. Cheap water power has been a major factor in Sweden's industrial development, and around 15% of the country's energy comes from hydroelectric plants. The vast forests of softwoods supply a highly developed sawmill, pulp, paper and finished wood product industry. Other manufactured products include high-quality steel, engineering products, chemical products, building materials, timber products, furniture, glass and china.

Media: Sveriges Radio runs three radio channels and Sveriges Television runs two TV channels. They are not government sponsored and are noncommercial. There are also regional TV and radio programs. There are 161 daily newspapers.

Education: A unified education system provides 9 years' compulsory schooling from the age of 7 to 16. More than 80% go on to two or more years at upper secondary school, and 25% of these continue to college or to a university. There are six universities.

Glossary

archaeologist Someone who studies the ancient remains of mankind.

elk A large deer, living in Northern Europe and Asia.

ghetto A densely populated part of a city, often inhabited by people who are socially deprived.

Gulf Stream The warm ocean current which flows from the Gulf of Mexico northeastward off the Atlantic coast to Northern Europe.

hydroelectric power Electricity produced by machinery driven by water power.

immigrant Someone who comes to a country to settle in it permanently.

inflammable Likely to catch fire.

integrate To merge a racial or religious group into a community.

konditori A bakery, confectionery and coffee-shop, all in one.

lumberjacks People who work at felling trees and transporting timber.

Lutheran Church The protestant community founded by Martin Luther, German leader of the Protestant Reformation in the sixteenth century.

migration The movement of animals at specific times of the year to new lands for fresh pasture etc.

NATO North Atlantic Treaty Organization — an organization of 15 countries formed for collective security.

nomads People who move from place to place, to find pasture, food or work.

neutral country A country that does not take sides with any other country in a war or dispute.

ordination The act of conferring holy orders when someone is accepted into a church as a clergyman.

ornithologist Someone who studies the behavior of birds.

pacifist A person who supports the belief that war is unjustified.

postmortem Examination of a body to find out the cause of death.

racist Holding the view that some races are superior to others because of their physical or cultural characteristics.

refugee Someone who has fled from political persecution in another country.

Sami The language of the Lapps, who live in the north of Sweden, Finland, Norway and the Soviet Union; also the name Lapps call themselves.

sexist Discriminating on the basis of sex.

snowmobile A motor vehicle for traveling on snow, fitted with caterpillar tracks and front skis.

theology The study of doctrines and religious beliefs.

United Nations An international organization of independent states formed in 1945 to promote peace and international cooperation and security.

Acknowledgments

The author would like to acknowledge the invaluable assistance of the Swedish National Tourist Office, The Swedish Institute, and DFDS Tor Line.

Photo Credits: Pages 10/11 Eivon Carlson; Pages 26/27 Bert Persson; Page 42 Barbro Carnehag

Index

j 948.5   NERL

Keeler, Stephen.

We live in Sweden

OCT.   1992

MAR   9 1990

DATE DUE

4 P APR '81				
APR 1 1981				
JUL 15 1981				
BGV APR '82				
LU OCT '84				
S1 HS MAY 86				

DEMCO 38-30T

ABC-2496

VERMONT DEPT. OF LIBRARIES

0 00 01 0497524 8